I0529815

backbeat ocean

poems by
janette kennedy

Backbeat Ocean
Copyright © 2022 JANETTE KENNEDY
All Rights Reserved.
Published by Unsolicited Press.
Printed in the United States of America.
First Edition.

No part of this book may be used or reproduced in any
manner whatsoever without written permission except in the
case of brief quotations embodied in critical articles or
reviews.

"Mudslide" originally appeared in *Tiferet Journal* blog.
February 20th, 2018.

"What Your Ticket Buys," "How to Build a Wall," "that
morning," "The Evolution of Play," "My Name," "A New
Wand," and "Afternoon Exhale" are all revised versions of
poems originally appearing online as a part of *Tiferet Journal*'s
poem-a-thon in April 2018.

Attention schools and businesses: for discounted copies on
large orders, please contact the publisher directly.

For information contact:
Unsolicited Press
Portland, Oregon
www.unsolicitedpress.com
orders@unsolicitedpress.com
619-354-8005

Cover Design: Kathryn Gerhardt
Editor: Bekah Stogner

ISBN: 978-1-956692-42-6

Some of these poems deal with trauma and mental health struggles. If you or someone you know is in crisis, please reach out to the National Suicide Hotline at 1-800-273-8255 or text HOME to 741741.

Poems

Sunlight

backbeat
ocean

Sunlight

Backbeat:

In the space after the downbeat:

conductor's flick and twirl,
repercussive balance shift after
the first earth cut, down

the space after
the sister of
the place next to

a sculptor's chiseled
emptied rock, now flung ricochet
into the universe

the picture bends beside
a flame
in deconstructed light

masseuse touch frees;
syncopated offbeat waves
replenish the vacuum gasp.

How Long?

How long does it take a people to learn their strength
is in the backbeat?

Space gives form, bulges
—and makes room.

Sanctuary

Part the curtains.
Obsidian rivers offset wispy willows.

Listen.
Guardian waterfalls murmur ear-tickle secrets.

Breathe.
Swirling breezes cool screaming sun shards.

Step in.

Who?

Who are your people?

Sculpted walkways approximate divinity
—brachiating pulse.

Who are your people?

Do they hide in the nook where the paths diverge,
waiting for the flow?

Do their bloody footprints step through alleys and over fences
in search of drum-breath vibrations?

Or somewhere further?

—meandering the hard scrapes on a cavern wall,
following mica veins and brain pick of salty rush,
shimmering beyond the flow.

Who are your people?

At You

A censored horizon heaves
salt-laced streams:
a wind rush to deliquesce nose-tips.

While knuckles-deep in wet sand
divining earth,
masters search salt flicks and sand fleas.

Anxiety

Calling it anxiety is such a silly thing.

What are you anxious about?

The question makes no sense—as if there was a thought, a
      moment I could
remember that sparked the propulsion zipping down the
      third rail of me.

My ancestor never stopped running.

Perhaps there's a wisdom she knows that I do not: that it's
still not safe, even though I tell her it's all okay now.

                  Isn't it?

She grabs my hand and guides me to the cliff—along the
edge—to balance me as I stretch fingertips to touch the
mist-christened minerals of forty-foot falls.

Silence

I want to ask,
Do you see the same patterns,
the same color of sky, as you did long ago?
But your toothy lipstick downbeat,
bassline pulse,
and liquid foundation that is anything but,
drums me back to silence.

On a wet day in February

Red berries hang
full from shadow
shrub tips.

Shadow Bait

Shadow side opposes sun,
though stays connected,
living in between inhale and exhale,
initiating neither.

And what if I travel off the asphalt,
step onto the half-grassed dirt
where mud and broken green bits
lodge in my tread?

Twilight

Plummet

Will you let me plummet,
slip-dive into gradient depths
where colors forget to breathe
and are satisfied to infiltrate,
saturate? Finger currents
play and lift my hair in tentacles
along the breadth of where I've been
and what I've left behind.

Clamshell

Survival holds the clamshell closed,
a tight fingertip pearl from a little hand
given over to me for safekeeping.

At home in a sandy lint pocket:
calcite sunset beach memory,
a gray-and-lavender-striped shroud.

Light Sluice

Cleanse the brilliant
light sluice rays wane to mere directions,
atoms slide by,
avoid the nothingness that once was churning
center

still, a dark impediment hole
leftover gravity glutton
breaks the universe.

Loose

Iridescent mica adorns fine-packed brick, bent beneath the heat that works to form utility in the spin. Twirling zooms, solid ephemera yields to the sculpting knife spilling out wormy swirls.

Were I to envision the paths of each trail, an artist watches a planet quicken between her hands, kinetic energy bound into the life of minerals. Water smooths the drying ledges and softens ridges, but does not solve this thirst, for the clay is shaky today.

Anticipation

the cut bud lingers in water;
ghost bloom,
going through the motions
even as petals
fall forward

Jazz:

Sauntering through the chilled fog of an autumn morning,
the wet smell of last night's campfires lingers in speckled
      breeze
between scarlet and amber, igniting the gray,
and takes bets to see which falls first.

The Gulf in Winter

Survivors come because the air is cold,

    the water ambivalent.

They can stand no more passion,

    no more heartbreaking joy.

The sun is a fake god,

    and summer is best served on ice.

Hypnogogic

Bump up,
cross tracks in one skipped beat.

What lies between mist-woven trees, through colander
curves?

Breaking Time

I'll know you
in the backbeat: blue
hydrangea blossom
seeps from acid-bathed roots.

I'll know you
in the rebound: restless
decay flings breath
backwards into the world.

I'll know you
in the tumult: time's
Fibonacci spiral
splinters to hold our space.

I'll know you
after the exhale: expired
lip-blown whispers
release incense rivulets to fly.

In the After

Do you live in the after
the lilt of release
the silence after the fan is turned off and the frost melted
but still the foggy tendrils rise,
and the radio just turned off,
the room, full of empty chairs
askew—

Loco Motive

There are too many songs about trains. With all the songs about trains, you would think them the pulse, or at least the pace, of a nation. So says the documentarian's narrative. Still though, the rumble. Even the underground's whine laces the pedestrian street. It's not like an airplane, so far off it easily blends into the background. The train though, the ground rumble distracts.

Tentacles

Undertow slices the waves backwards.
Abyss sends her tentacles out,
reaching for life in the sunlit water
but succeeding only in the rip current drown.

As waves ebb,
windswept streams rise
pulling effervescent lace across lit sand
so that now we can walk
between teal stripes
across the water.

Dark blankets stretch out
shadow-laden underbellies hang low
in a solemn-storm lullaby to shield us from the sunlit day
wetting the reeds
evoking our slime coats
and salty-sea lizard dreams.

jam

sad days seep from the citrus press
above boiled strawberry summer
evaporating,
steam returns the favor.

The Space You're In

Look at the space you're in
what was once here, before you?
what is here now?

What could be tomorrow if your dreams come true and
hammer and nail align
in well-appointed design?
—but if they don't,
or maybe one day, even if they do—
what clicking, crawling creatures,
shoots and fronds,
primordial must
will retake the space when you look away?

Fog

Early February fog, like wings

speak speak

sailboats in stream,

a misplaced summer opens

the unconscionable dream.

Manatee

It happens as it always has:
unexpectedly.

In the daily scans for dolphin arcs or the quick slip slice of
how the movies said sharks would come,

as if we could outrun them if they were coming for us.
it happens next to,
between,
unseen,
until it is not.

Falling

Dusk-lit dreams toss echo grenades on seaside balconies,
salted-lace wisps clarify stars,
bay lights turn red to save sea turtles,
and smoky teal strata coax indigo horizon
so I could fall off the earth to the synchronized breaking of
    waves.

Fear

I walk the perimeter
bind up the shadow's boundary,
crusty baked edges
of necessity,
groveling a step below hope

gasping above
what lies below the growing shadow:
measures of small-batch cupcakes,
frosting drips down the drain
because we are all sick of the sugar.

Lurking forward
beyond my reach,
choices not my own
will always be the whole of me
as she bites in.

Midnight

What Anger

What anger speaks the hidden world
and keeps the darkness large
so even the softest light
makes it hurt to see?

Strength

strength slithers beneath waves
letting the beating calls drift on and ricochet off
blood-hued canyon walls

Between

Between you and me—
walls built around window intention

but at night
refractory moonlight
steps through shadow space
and afterthoughts

Turn Off

Is it wrong to turn off the day?
To say it is *enough*—
let us hide and rest
until we are ready
to return
as us.

Self-care

They tell us to practice self-care, to do something every day for ourselves. I have to question their motives, though. It looks nice on the surface—a lie of retreat, coping. But still, checking off an endless list of tasks.

Is it enabling? Allowing the rest of the world to sell my wholeness back to me?

What if everything I did all day, each day, was for me?
I would feed you because I want your health.
I would reach out for me.
I would retreat for me.

What Your Ticket Buys

House lights down,
guitar in hand
wearing boots scuffed raw
from last year's hits,

he would sing the song:
the one that everyone for twenty years
had told him never to sing
in public.
Yes, he would sing.

His callouses strummed
the whiny old dirge
that landed like knives
on our ears,
a grating song
thrusting his frayed soul
onto the stage.

Cutting Board

stretch reach knife slice
through scallion green tips
moist white disks
a million cuts on wood flesh
release pungent drift.

Aging Rebellion

Methodical cogs in well-
ordered systems, facilitate
blustery creativity's knell.
Half-shorn trees anticipate

the remaining fall
before the still air
of winter's icy scrawl,
portending the heirs

of smokestack days: in
grand smiling style,
fear and his twin,
predictability, while

in fragrant wisps,
my heart remembers
when chaos
held it together

and the train rumble
made it explode.

I'm getting swallowed

I thought it would be a boa constrictor winding her way around me and swallowing me whole. I thought I wouldn't like it very much. The slow progression from toe to middle was supposed to be terrifying.

I wonder now, though, if, that way, I could at least stay together, not flayed into a thousand pieces by over-and-over-again lists. The last minute—always it's the last minute—race against the clock to keep things perfect, or at least as expected, and, hopefully, as it's supposed to be.

They didn't tell me that I would fall apart racing across the rocks as a blinded archer shoots arrows at the stars, disintegrating before I even get to see where the arrow lands.

And there, in a million little pieces of confetti and glitter, my last breath of sinewy muscles turns to ash, not leaving nearly enough for the boa constrictor to bother with.

Who knew?

Who knew you then—
with your big-eyed song that never thought not
to turn the sticky handle or pull against a closed door?

Who knew you where the circles met
and conjunctive phrases always brought everything back
        around,
when spiderwebs were dreams?

The bits, sporadic

the bits, sporadic
like balloon rain
drop, bouncing off in ecstasy

or

sharp-sleet infirmity,
the iron shell of a focused train
barreling down the well-planned track

unfolds into wings,
sails slicing sky,
open-air glider

or maybe

it's an ocean today
and I, a clumsy submarine,
negotiate mines tethered to the ocean floor

grasping for something
to give shape to the space
I travel through

Abyss

Supposed to

I'm supposed to be wise.
I'm old enough.
Resigned, maybe.
At peace.
Not endlessly done—still!—with the barrage
as if there is redeeming value
to continuing whatever façade has made attention
my wealth and poverty.

Facebreak

You will not see me in pixels.
I live in icy breath incense murmurs.
Faces break open in rocket confetti
that sparks a flipside fire
to spotlight a curtain-strewn stage.

sky pull

She holds heaven in a kite string
where billow turn and release
coax a bony knuckle ride
and sanguine pulses waltz with breath swells.

Swift freedom, gust liberation.
Lost, the handle skips and glides
just beyond her earthbound cells,
scraping beachgrass spikes.

Sand cups her knees.
In rocksalt kisses,
she grieves
the sky pull.

How to Build a Wall

away from this dark spring
where angels seek their recompense
where it hurts to heal
and guilty are the oblivious

dig big holes into the ground

"something hurts," the fires cry,
releasing blood into the sky

set the posts straight and tall

"something hurts," the smokes rise
and we cover our eyes so they don't tear up
because, in the end, it's all really too much
and everybody hurts anyway

let the cement harden around them

"something hurts," so off we go,
behind the walls to what we know
to shelter in our platitudes
and forget the rectitude
as if it's already too late

bang in the fire-forged iron bars

too late to cry
too late to look
too late to feel
so all that's left is really thus:

fasten the wood impenetrable

and wonder why the sun forgot to rain

but if the walls succumb,
your bubble might pop
you free

The Memory of Monsters

We bumble along on secured hay bales. Sipping cocktails of
chilled air, we forget our ancestors took it for granted.
Catfish stock the pond, swimming too eagerly around the
outskirts, as evenly-spaced evergreen saplings pretend to
be wild. A fountain gushes in the center of this world,
endlessly flinging borrowed water into the glittering sun.

Still, Gaia infiltrates.

A wrinkled clay-ancient grandmother of mineral-flecked
soil and agate veins feeds the pumpkin patch and the
worms, bathing the potbellied pig with her mask. We allow
her in these filtered bits before the children return to their
cinderblock classrooms, before we catch the train that fuels
the cities, where it used to be that disembodied gorgon
faces, swirling eyes on gates and armor, invoked the
memory of monsters.

Shadow eyes searched for me, cloaked in the night outside
my window. I hid between the trapezoids of filtered
streetlight, flayed out across the path between my bed and
the bathroom. I asked her, "Why did you give us these
monsters?"

So what is it then that swims beneath the city? Where
water seeps below and drips into sewers flowing effluent,
an albino ribbed back slides along the surface, blind in

underground toxic waste, slithering through the capillaries of a city, undetected.

pietas

What if I
touched the sacred stones
that remember you,
expressions chiseled by ancient hands,
instructing me in martyrdom,
placed in holy chapels?

would they be warm
and wet
like the stones of Aleppo,
dripping with the blood
of children?

Infinity Mirrors, 2017.

Two eyes look back at me as our house pulses large and
small in them. Into the depths of birds swimming and fish
flying, I ask if there is hope. When the green goes, will the
red remain? Lava flows into our souls, cauterizing what
was left of our bloody, beating hearts. The sounds of trains
that used to calm my worried mind with their earth-rush
are now the footsteps of giants smashing trees and
breaking up the rock shale that we once built our lives on.
Water turns to fire in the age of Aquarius as parched
swollen tongues drown in the salty sea rise. And I, with my
hopeful little eyes, see eternity in one little slip of a tear.
The hospital doors reveal a womb inside. Blood-filled cords
feed the living and battle with beeps and heartbeats against
weakening, dying flesh that gasps along the edge of
primordial oblivion. Where policemen accost the nurses
who dare to stand up and say no, so that we need
policemen for policemen and rules just for the men who
make the rules about the womb and then accost it. Even
while people are dying and others are fighting to heal
them, unseen. The river hangs in the air, raising the corpse
of DeSoto, who ravaged the natives and whose men sunk
his corpse in the Mississippi so no one would know he
wasn't a sun-god. So since he's up, let's drive a stake
through his brain and bury him next to Nathan Bedford
Forrest in the city that if it could, would squeeze out both
of them, white pus from a teenage pimple to splatter in
blood-laced sinewy streaks across the mirror I lean into.

Hurricane

Rain-spiked air hovers above the bones basted in tropical spice beneath a local sand coating. Laying all open before birds return, floodwaters turn to stew, and fractal worms creep up saturated sheetrock

—what a name, sheets of rock, as if I could crawl into the earth and pull the granite over me for a cool slumber

But even that is false.

Death does not do the rotting. It's life that rots the remnants and thus takes care of itself, regardless of what bright-eyed sentience happens to join the fray.

Sleep, Once and Forever

Sleep done right
zoetrope adventures
through the night
means waking
body light.

Three slow winks,
a body releases
mind over brink,
drifting as
the world slinks.

Icarian Mirror

I love Icarus. Watching him fly so high and then fall reminds me, as I sit in the depths of the plummet, that flying, too, is dangerous…and that maybe, if he flies so high that he falls down, I can go so deep, I will fall up.

Save the Ocean

Flexibility succumbs to age in important things, like sight
and wineskins, attempting to hold back the burgeoning
new for the sake of support, security, as if stasis was ever
the way of the world. For millennia, the ocean beat pounds
against ancient shores rolling with slick fins, tempering
winds into currents.

But now, too, the sea ages in the hidden places, cracking
into microplastic fusion, where eternal abyss finds a floor,
stasis rises to overtake the ancient ways, covered in
unwitting waste from the landgods above.

Hadal

Darkness

Sometimes,
darkness
forgets to exhale
and only
swells.

Waiting Game

"What time is it, Mister Fox?" the morning
school bus stop sings. Gazelle steps and bobbing bright
      eyes leap over chasms between days,
legs ready to take flight, if only wings
would comply.

An abandoned oven in a backfield anticipates a house unbuilt.
Rust creeps along its edges. Overgrown seed tips flirt with flaky
white paint, caressing an itch.

Hampered shadow strides jostle
between sun slices, hoping
to remain unseen. Numbers gamble
someone else will be slower or closer
when Fox turns around.
They measure steps
together: days
corralled into lists and obligations.

Dreams flee to a rusty bus tucked alone among pristine Alaskan
wilds, where something nutritious, like wild potato seeds, becomes
toxic to a body that is starving.

Nearly negligible steps shuffle
through strewn crackling leaves,

huddle close, wait, afraid
teeth will turn and barrel down.

Still they whisper,
"What time is it, Mister Fox?"

that morning

before
the stars' last-gasp dawn
she did not see the bend
where blood-soaked newspapers
soon would lay strewn
on the not-yet-dewy grass
their corners flicked
by a gusty wake
over a mangled bike

if only
a glint
or a flutter
or a falling cigarette lighter
had summoned her
swerve

Bog Body

They came to see me off, like a spectacle. You know they did. The fire was too bright that night, the noise too loud. Once more let me feel the night air on my face without this braided cord around my neck or leather cap on my head. Nothing is ever so cold as the moment you know you'll never be clothed again.

Earth enveloped me in her acid sweat. Preserved for eternity, almost, by the cold human hands that sliced my neck open, and let my blood seep into the soil. It was a relief I guess, to brave the cackles and reverie. To succumb, and have it be done.

It's always been that way, the pulsing, beating wet goo that gives life to one, and sucks it out of others. The bog took my bones, but left my skin. So you still get to see my face, the cord around my neck, my humanness, my nakedness. And so that you don't get to believe that you are anything but me.

A Million Deaths

Tonight, you die a million deaths.
Accusations stab at your soul,
publicly beat you breathless.
Multitudes desperately seek
redemption from you
and death to you.

Figures sit afar,
waiting in the sky,
drifting into darkness.
As light from your warrior robes,
thrust mockingly upon your shoulders,
reflects on mother and child.

No really, tonight, you die a million deaths.
Whatever divinity that refuses to let this cup pass
also refuses you
dignity, swiftness, and morphine,
requiring one long march
through human agony.

Seconds wane slowly when neurons scream.
The body fights to heal, clawing for hope,
waiting for the mind to figure some other way out of this

damn thing.
Powerful men wash their hands of it, overcome by
        shadows,
divinities turn away.
And you are given up to the process of the day.

That ancient mob knows it's never really been about the
        end,
but drawing out the process.
Like the sisters who snip, the end belongs to divinities.
It is their plaything.
While we who are left walk the long march,
the procession of the day.

Caregiving Fog

"What speaks?" Picnic tuna sandwiches bemoan blurred-out fleshy smiles.

"The birds," you say. "On their way south to heaven's gate."

There, at last, I dream.

In church, I look too long without blinking and watch the grainy rainbow of my dry eyes dissolve my vision.

Dried-out leaves float on the pond's surface, spices added too late to the stew on a lukewarm day.

The body of the boy, my classmate, is found a day after his fishing skiff on the grassy banks of a brackish Tidewater bay. His smiling face must have been lifeless with mouth agape, like my grandfather's was when they carried him out of our house.

Our house is full of shadows: the dark blue of drawn shades and windowless hallways. Stomping through the Great Dismal Swamp, the wilderness exculpates our curses. We offer up tuna sandwiches to an abandoned dog. Dark as night, she sleeps in the deepest part of our hallway, where shadows animate and coalesce when we trip over her. Colors tumble to black, bind us in the spectrum.

Living between the lights, I listen to my grandmother's last breath through a cracked door. I kiss her still-warm pliable hand before they usher me out again.

We fling our bikes where the street turns to dust and climb into abandoned sewer pipes. When the high school kids come, they bang out drum solos on our hiding place and rock the pipe. We will, we will, rock you. Tumbling over each other, our skin skids along the metal ridges. Jagged edges slice and tear as the sun sets, so that only a slice of crescent pain is left to light our way home through the fog.

Child's Play

I killed them—
shot them all dead—
so I could get to the next level.

siblings took turns
looking over shoulders
at *killed* and *shot.*

silence frayed her belt.
her hair, braided knots with beads,
clicked against each slow turn

until her brother tickled her
and the one person in the world who could,
pulled her back from the blood-pooling front yard memory

Seaward

Elliptical covers employ fascinations
in cycles to destroy conglomeration.

Into the void, extremity.
Return to me, antipathy
and on beyond the crescent dream
a fixated boar retrieves the scene
and passes into never-want
where all the rest of us are not.

Folded trials spring the teal
into grace's open seal
where never did I think or want
about a grievous juggernaut
so slips the spit of tarried pride.
Oh, give us all good, on the side.

Ancient sparks of hidden dew
fold the flowers good and true
thus speaks the big ole featherweight
of love, "admonish hate."
Will soon there be eternity
into the grove of me

or else did any flick or seal entrust
the biopic zeal
of you and me and all the rest
until the story lies (at my behest)?
Angel speaks the biggest song
into the feeling days, go long

there the seaward sun will flee
into the realm, eternity.
where once a host of daffodils
did speak their ancient trill
'til now there is no sign or rest.
Where an emerging song vest

opens as truth is finally told:
the wise old man thus did fold.

Hope:

Stilted orange knives lean against smoking rough spots.

Icy fingertips stretch out:
      believe fire will warm blood as it makes its last turn before retreat to the pumping core.
      believe fire will break down undigestible peptide bonds into salty tender bites.

Yet, the greedy hearth spits disaster so easily in one errant consummating spark.

Train Death

The train that killed you
still rushes over the molecules of your mangled flesh.

It's not that it didn't want to stop.
It just couldn't.

And the engineer
still panics, wishing he had somehow known.

Reversed the fire of mechanized motion.
Turned physics upside down.

Half-Drawn Unicorn: elegy for an artist

Hoof tip angle
steps over.
Red and yellow strokes dissolve into space
and so, also, their cache of indigo night.
Masquerade white,
the underbelly shine of deep spectrum
nebula bath. Lines unclosed
curve and twist into what is—
lost.

elegy for an artist (revised)

Hoof tip angle steps through
sun-soaked zag—racing light.
Eviscerate the sky until it bleeds out blue,
dissolve the cache of indigo sight.
Giant nebulae underbellies shine
in masquerade white.
Empty lines upraised swirl and curve
around what would have been
more than pigment on paper—
but, now, is lost.

elegy for an artist (revised again)

negative space leaves nothing to chance—it's forever
      unknown.

You might think the natural point of entry is a convex
      horn tip, but not to the artist, who builds the
      picture from a tuft of ear hair
or some other unexpected place. Left unfinished,
the artist's gestalt leaves nothing
to chance.

elegy for an artist (the end)

An unfinished life left lines drifting in space.

Talisman

Don't worry.
I won't leave you here.
Always the surface remains above
the depths below.

eternity

Barometer shift pressure plummets
a whirlpool pulls
and then avalanche hordes
in mountain winds
creep up
so forearms and fingers vanish,
dance in and out of real
flashing teleport to seared memory
when I held you, unable to feel me
and your sweet little heartbeat
frolicked for a moment
with eternity.

Mudslide

Danger brings us here, where experts smile and say, "Just a little more time." In their swagger, we let our secret seed out into the open to bloom. It is a strong plant, with tendrils strong enough to hold us as we climb over the steep rocks.

This day, added to the next and the next after that, will get us somewhere. We believe it in the dew-chilled mornings, holding the darkness at bay, and in the rough evenings when callouses give way and bleed.

The tendrils grow stronger, lift us up and turn us over as we dare to gaze up at the sky and dream.

We climb the mountain. Our dirt-filled brows drip with fog as we pull ourselves over the crest to find a wind-whipped barren land. The experts grow wings and take flight, while the vines around us shrivel.

I have nothing left to give you, and so I take your hand as the mudslide of this life rumbles us down. No one comes for us that night, as the mud cakes our bruised bloodied bodies.

A tear trickles down and waters your hand in mine, as if it were a seed.

Abyss

Taking the Plunge

Sometimes, I want to plunge a knife below my sternum.
Not to end my life, but to touch the hurt.

Sometimes, I think I must be alone in that feeling because if
everyone else felt it too, then surely, collectively, we would
not have the strength to go on.

But then, I hear a beat in a bring-back-blues-simple sigh,
see rock and space flow together in sweeping sculpted cry,
watch a whisper shadow grow onto canvas as spectrum
explodes.

And I know I am not alone.

Poem Spider

One black line slinks into view,
watching the night waves flit and flutter until the flailing
      sticks.

Tightly wound web stills,
a quick jab to melt heart and bone.

She waits, ready to suck life in.

Split Open

They stood in the aisle, connecting perfumes and umbrellas. Their voices merely peppered lips when we walked by, as if the telling itself would infect.

But already, I know. I go down to the depths and I know you've been there, too, in the moments I fold in.

I saw you, marching on a misplaced mud-frozen day between toys and fire-engine Santa. A reconvened curb with a splattering of children, and you—your numbers reduced by one—belted out a Christmas crescendo mourning wail, seeking no more light, just love.

I come back from the depths with the same song as you split open me. Let loose the song between.

Folding

The cape usually encompasses my wake, drifting and flying off. But now, in dawn's early stealth, the fabric covers me in layers and breathes in quiet whispers to seal the seam that has begun to fray.

Stolen

There was part of you that still wanted this life—I know it—and even though, all-consuming and felt in a vacuum, hope's fickle flame used up all the air.

Were you like me? Did the monsters in your head refuse to sit down this time; did they forget to burn themselves out? Did they run ramshackle out of control, trailing your body along? Were you there on the tracks trying to catch up to the stampede that had already stolen you?

The Tree that Gave Birth

They knew it was coming in the smell of cracked cedar and wet broken pine. It came from between the cracks where bark split and tumbled over itself—out of the rings of experience: the thick fat ones and slivers of dry years. It came from all of them together. The creature emerged in tendril flight, caught hold of the storm coming in, and stopped for a time in the bare winter branches, captive between what was home and foreign. She pushed beyond what could be known, bleeding skin against the rough bark which had made the tree so strong and once was protection.

The Evolution of Play

flip down, spin, swirl
line the figures up
just so
knees scrape on a
backwards slide
frustrated
cold nose run
fingers chip and
bend rules, imagine
spectrum blur
bookend school days
a reason to finish,
a purpose, "what if"
fashion ways to keep shadows at bay
in restful release
memories entice—
connect, distract, interact
fluid norms
hope contorts into purpose
two colors emerge as life settles
into opposing ends
play and work
totter between
escape shadows

                                        settle into scratchy
safe wool
                            convergent hurricane
                                    glass obscures a brief
oil-lamp flicker
                                                remember
divergence
                                                    cage
lift
                                                    dial
turn, wick raise,

        grow flame, grow

        transform shadows.

I suppose

I suppose that
- I should feel safe driving home in between landscapes that comply with the character of the neighborhoods.
- the lit fountain should inspire something in me on walks at night with my dog.
- the playground should assuage concern.
- the distant high school marching drums should be enough beat in my soul.
- the walking trail that greens my life with wild dreams should suffice.
- the networks of highways and shallow roots should supplant my dreams of earth-connecting caves, the negative millennia of fire pits surrounded by hewn stones.
- if I had roots more than a couple hundred years old, something in me would belong.

I can trace an ancestor back to England in 1200-something, and a pilgrim, too, but England doesn't feel like home.

Home is on the banks of this river: the mud that flows rich mineral silt between us bringing your tears to me.

What's home is the dark in me you've always seen, and never been afraid of.

Ode to a Gas Station Bathroom

What is ugly,
but a speckled mirror in a gas station bathroom,
peeling caulk, and petroleum-infused morning sweat
to frame transience.

It's the moment I could change,
if I dared to drop layers of UV-filtered glasses
and pus-glazed contact lenses. I could step out,
unhinge the door, let the mildew stains bleach
in the sun.

But alas, the gas station is not my own.
Tears slip from the faucet
pulling moldy slivers with them,
but still, I embrace the flittering shadows
of what I see in the mirror.

Blues:

Release seaweed tendrils into waves
where kraken glides—
waits with hydra tentacles
to meet them, flailing
in a dance through lost depths,
the pus-crusted shore line
seals the scar of a worn-out wound.

My Name

My name means "God's gracious gift," like Joan of Arc,
prophetic warrior—sounds like a bit much. Except it's not
when absence comes: I realize. in the depths of a broken
sky, this screaming puncture wound of light, chaotic nebula
mess, is infinitely beautiful, even if it is not.

charred frame tethers sweat
incense prayers rise, groaning cold,
still, I blow slowly,
determined last ember, flakes
fly into eyes, burning grace.

Memory of Fire

Old wet leaves wait for months. Between the seasons, the solstice poles beckon and stretch us, playing the vibrating breath of a rubber band stretched around the henge, raising the pitch so maybe we can hear, and not just the earth.

Except it never was about our ears anyway as we slip along the lines between cogs and try to get our bearing in the stars. Heavenly hands pluck and play, but the solstice simply pulls and spins us on its way. It never was supposed to rain today.

In January, I forgot what snow felt like. It drifted down around me, but I could not feel it. I reached out, but it melted the instant I touched it. So there was only the soft, wet mildewed smell of a forgotten fire pit, abandoned after the last grilling of the season. The earth heaves as it turns like the horizon breathing, and I wonder if it won the race or climbed as far as it was hoping to. I dream of the ocean, but maybe that's just a salty armpit filling with seaweed before the razor comes. The lightning flash that says, you know you never did belong, slicing through the root that keeps me tethered. But then, there's the wet smell of smoke hanging in the air, infiltrating my hair and daring me to believe that, come the dry season, a forest could ignite me.

A Lost Smith

What happens to the hatch-battened forge still burning?
What tools are set aside as billows enflame
and lungs succumb?
When did you decide to forego restless freedom in a
        nighttime chill?
Remaining instead inside the smoky room,
can you ever dare to quench
the fire that comforts and consumes?

In Telling

hair wisp Icarian halo
melted into bowed wings

ember-laced charcoal
births invisible incense flight

released feathers slip
to sickle-sliced space

half-lit tales ignite travels
through smithy's hammer pummels

and thus, a fiery snake bends her own flying wisps
before hardening into form

Inverted

A speckled mind glides behind mirrored sunglasses
through scenes of out-of-sync staccato ticks.
Shadows diverge. Mixed-up time
slips by.

Stingy humid despair,
refuses rain.

Light ends upside down,
against the back of a brain,
soaked into electric matter,

Passion ends inverted,
yearns for a quiet slip to misty clouds,

infiltrating cells.

drifting cool and wet
among helical
falcons.

A New Wand

Dew slice, intricate grass shadows
toss back the daybreak light
and laugh in glinting grins. Piercing polka dots push
against logs, scaly charred wet ash infiltrates whispers,
she reaches into yesterday's waste,
slips a knife along the verge
but leaves a scraggly, blackened edge
to honor the forging of a new wand.

Midnight

Decompression

Swift ascension jolts scaly skin into a well-appointed
dress code hanging haphazard.
Shallow breath against minuscule pocket hordes
emerges from and catches within, paralyzed,
hidden, and bound beneath time contortion.

Drift

return to life slowly
breathe into the backbeat
and know me there

Destruction

A pillar toppled in a midnight rip, felled by wind and soupy mud leeching strength from tired roots. Decades of woodpecker holes and washed-out lightning scars rest now in earthen wounds, as leaves and worms rush in—white blood cells, to heal, inflame.

heaven's pillar crash
against earth in Spring storm's breath
freeing nutrients

Decaying leaves confront their old comrades who were left behind to ride the demise. All together again, splinters whisper tales of fluttering breezes to the soil that years ago had fed the seed and sapling. And so, the tree nurtures back the earth it once grew from.

wind's breath rumble drum
bangs the giant's crashing rage
break stories open

Dark Spinning

sparkle silk encodes moon-gilt core
fills meandering crevices in a carefully constructed wall
that some earth shift or mud swallow compromised to
Arachne's fate:
too many legs splayed beneath too many eyes
maneuver in bulbous iridescence,
consume wineskin brew of sticky beat paralysis,
click,
satiate,
retreat,
release restless night wisps to dabble residue
and beckon auroral dawn.

Ancient Winds

postmortem
galaxy propellants
bathe us in dark matter
winds unseen
cloak the stars and slip
through sliding shadows

dimensions

limbs eschew a hardened back
built-in dimensions of want
as if to say the ocean dreams
have passed their torch to forest scenes
where eyes that glow amid the night
explore the tantric demon's flight

What Ghost?

What ghost did you leave
that drew birds pulling branches,
playful before the rain
pelting my car like pennies
falling from the sky for luck?

Night Sheets

Shushing night sheets
the river tells me to sleep
but still, I step in. Soft billows become
icy tethers pulling me any way
but forward.

Between us,
snotty tears drip fear
as boulders buffet
us around a swirling current
to open the world,

but still together pulling
we are at once
risking loss
and risking
all.

Split

When was it that you learned to split yourself in two?

When you realized it was the thickness of the glass keeping you safe from the faces peering in?

When it occurred to you that the forest exists without you and beyond your bedroom window is a deep, dark night with glittering pinpricks of light?

Reflections on a Tree

It spoke to the sky with fists upraised
nearly a million of them:
complicated branches twisting, searching for light
covering up and growing around
the dead parts.
Pecked holes embroider broken shards scraping the skies.

The branches cannot be untangled
perhaps I could
if I could climb that high.
one day, though,
the water swell will loosen its roots
the ground will shake
and this paralyzed tree will explode the ground
with life.

Blueberry Tithe

Misplaced frost
made the blueberries late this year;
Some say they may not come at all.
Most likely though, on a Tuesday
we'll pick some wet pieces of thunder-broken sky,
and taste sweet bursts rolling on tongues.
The blue brethren slip easily from agitated branches,
anointing the ground.
Slow kiln heat seep awakens minister bees,
boils the fallen into jam,
and feeds a soil that has so long forgotten
what is sweet and blue.

nomad home

Inside insulated walls, air filters suffocate. The food will
kill you with traces of greed. Hydrogenated souls smile
from creaky eyes and doors grow thicker with clean, tight
hinges as giants reduce your dreams to electric snow
globes turned upside down.

Get back to your tribe:
the one that sings, one that chants
one full of happenstance,
one that moves.

Hope Revised

I will give you my hope. I don't really need it anymore.

It's not like my favorite pair of jeans,
with a story for each splotch of paint,
worn thin with holes in all the wrong places to be hip.

Or the black honeycomb Henley
I would wear with everything if I could,
a small constant pressure against my skin saying, "here you
        are."

It's not like the cold cry of morning,
chilling my coffee on contact
and milking tears from my eyes.

It's like the necklace I got,
all glittery with jade striations on a rock-solid back.
I could fall in love with it if I wanted to.

But then, I would have to hold on.

Hope Revised Again

Keep it safe, though.
Because when my children are grown
far beyond the realm of me,
I may ask for it back.

Twilight

Sadness

She comes and sits next to me, quiet
as if always
but never,
not really,
only sometimes,
but each time,
it feels like always forever more.
That is what she whispers.
I pat her knee and say it's okay
because I know there is no chasing her away.
If I avoid, she only yells louder and we are both lost in a
smoke-filled swirl.
We are patient friends
who need not speak,
only simply allow
rest in the suspended moment
of a pendulum swing.

Hidden

Hidden
in a tree nook, unseen life
peers out.

a breath

Breathe in—
deep down to fractal core swell
until so much discomfort
forces release
push life out, until tears and nose tinge
overtake the sacrifice
and once more,
breathe in.

I knew you

I knew you then,
intimately on the stage,
the you that hovered and swirled through your arms and
eyes
but now, when you cut avocados
and the layers of life fall upon you,
you are only human.

Ancient

I love you like the ancient sky.

Why do you use ancient so much?

It feels more real—mineral-based muck validates the
resiliency of the stuff that survives—a glimmer that could
      have been lost,
but yet remained.

Specter

The rumor's wake fans outward as silence glides between swimmers. In calm seas, they confront fear from comb jellyfish aggregation, gatekeepers to clear teal oscillating gulf waters. A daring child perhaps, but most likely the swift happenstance of a brush on a leg or an arm, indicates that these jellies will not sting. Primordial harbingers, they present each swimmer with the specter of her own fear, daring her to step in, slide past the gelatinous prehistory laying itself out: a warning. But oh, the euphoria of making it to the other side, beyond each slimy skid until the main cloud of jellies is left behind among the breakers.

Boulder Release

This morning's upheaval tossed safety to the fire,
confusion reigned stalwart beneath thick air,
rolling Sisyphean rock again

in despair I give up:

I stop to watch the road shift and slip.
Buttercups brush against leaning electric wooden poles.
The wonder-laced zephyr meanders among my post-rain
scented tears.

Eddies

Children cascade, tumble down itchy green bluffs,
ear over ear,
squeal over hair,
until alighting in spins by too-close cars zooming down
        Riverside Drive.

Breathless races seek steep slope, again. Hands pull spiky
        overgrown
ragweed, crushing
dandelions. Sparkling
eyes glitter, the evening air swirling through lung ache.

Golden hues drip into the river's welter whirl
bluster currents.
Ribbons whip
past open ears carrying the pulse of bicycle clicks.

Loosened breath, background bass, attends an ancient flute
        song,
sees churning tears,
blood mud,
growing the goo that festers, not yet rinsed in the sea.

Crocodile Dreams

A time capsule breaks open
submerged sunlight, glistening drops
fall to shadowed indigo
beneath a molten flame.

I ride a crocodile up into the dawn,
amidst golden glitter wave-peaks.
Mosaic-leathered edges measure me
in knuckle-flesh scratches
as we rise to face the fiery sky, descending.

Battle Within

What lives inside your saunter?
What drives the breath of steps?
Which cavern hides luminescence just beyond the next
      dark turn?
When you slip, which mineral sliver will slice the skin?
What germs will trigger T-cells to fight the battle within?

Complexity

The morning embraces
and runs her sweaty fingers along my arms,
through my hair, enlivening
follicles with an itch
to match the waves
of basal cicada song
flowing where water once did
across pumped-out lake bed.

Her fingernails scratch, impatient desire,
assuaging breeze caress.

Night Thoughts

Crepuscular drifts
brush canticles
in wind chimes
and breathy staccato sifts chill, feather tickles.

Soft hands
add lavender honey
milk warmth
to tall bands of percussive branches.

The coming storm
wrangles the night
scraping fondant
from a half-baked norm spread across messy faces.

Clamshell Eel

Translucent pink fins flow around a red eel core. I'm good at holding the clam mouth closed, keeping the oversized pincer inside. So good, I crack it in my fear and pulverize a fleshy, pink brain. My favorite dish towel becomes the shroud.

I don't expect it to come back, floating downstream out of corrugated metal pipe on sewer waste. Nor do I expect it to take flight as it does still beneath the towel shroud, translucent pink escaping the flapping edges.

You wrestle it as I did. But you don't hold the mouth shut. You are kinder; you appreciate its power. Whether from love or grace, you intentionally risk the pincer's clamp, rescue us all, and find it an enclave in a deep-sea forest.

It is then, at a safe distance, knowing it is in its appropriate depth, that my fear dissipates, becomes fascinated. I seek out the seaweed forest to feel the powerful current mouth, brave the pincer, appreciate pink flowing robes, and honor a primal red core.

Light Sometimes

I forget sometimes that I need your light, the garish multicolored blinking that doesn't keep away darkness or infiltrate my soul, but simply, in its blinking, keeps the world turning. Which might otherwise stop.

Sunlight

Above and Below

Skin breaks the surface, an open mouth climb
ambivalent light plays between sparkling wavelets
drops glisten in channels back to the sea.

Hand over hand, climb the rock face of grit and growth.

A sun beckons new, now only,
warms blood freed from scraped flesh
to fall and dissipate in salted flood,
as if there will be more.
Above and below,
always.

Fallen Pickets

A broken fence along the too-busy road sits shielded
behind an overgrown thick forest so that even if there is a
house somewhere in there, no one could ever see the
damaged parts. I see them, though, when I wait to join the
river of traffic rolling through cut hills around
embankments. Brick pillars hold two splintered two-by-
fours, unsure of their purpose now with bold fallen pickets,
leaving a window into the undergrowth forest behind,
either an escape or entry.

escargot

clingy escargot
adore slow oscillation
beats on seagrass cliffs

Real Wake

The smell of spring lingers after closing the windows,

the smell of *real,*

like when the gods close the doors of Olympus after a
human has trespassed and wafts of mortality linger.

Sandbar Mourning

A sickle sandbar touches the shore, beckons a walk on water, and offers up a waterlogged cornucopia of sea cucumbers as a mother carries an urn in the crook of her arm.

He steps across. Salt sand splashes on rolled woolen cuffs. His hand reaches back to her in her dark maroon mourning tights, funeral skin. Shoes cast off, she steps across. Ocean and sand seep into her filtering fabric.

Later in the hotel, mineral mud exfoliates her abrasion-rimmed toes. Bloody pink skin stings against each step.

Spring Night Emergence

Tangy tinges infiltrate slime
muck thaw ribbons dissolve and open unfrozen
like soft sugar lemon ice goddess blessings
possibility dancing in open space

evening exoneration

globs of razzmatazz watermelon peach jazz
trail along lips
and slimy mirror kisses,
obscuring the crone glimpse
of gleaming purple bit-littered face lines.
dark-lit hues unravel the last braid,
fluttering curtains whisper incantations
to soothe volcanoes and swingset blisters.
half-painted nails anointed by glitter
dissolve the sacred day,
so waxing gibbous sheets absorb contrite folds,
and chaos becomes a pixie dust ghost
haunting resilient night with pinprick reflector zing.

Afternoon Exhale

expectant gasp quickens
diesel engine scoff
brakes squeal to stop
children tumble off

little heads race home
the bus pulls away
afternoon waves
fall into play

all is okay

Petri Dish

A sweaty woolen overcoat
bakes, still wet,
releasing
yesterday's
labor's
moldy scent
into oversized dreams,
the ones that hover
just above slippery
fermenting sprouts.

Opening a tree

A tree once figured large in our yard,
with resilient lightning scars,
moss-covered bends,
and scraggly-framed woodpecker holes.
Looking up from below,
its branches crisscrossed the sky.

Such trees don't fall in just one night.
It takes months of rain to overwhelm the roots,
persuade them to release their grip,
just for tonight. Crashing splinters
create whole new habitats for earthworms who had yet to
taste the sky and the sun shakes hands with its old friend,
        the ground.

The workers carved it up and ground the stump,
but not before we saw the hollows that had been hiding
        within.
When the last behemoth bit is taken away,
the sun baptizes new seedlings.

Reclaimed Love

The wood on the coffee shop counter top holds a plaque that says it's reclaimed. Brought back from an obsolete use, presented now new in your need.

Except it's still wood, and one day, the counter will not be needed anymore. Or perhaps it will be, in a far-future museum, unused.

It will still be wood, though.

Even if you paint it to look like metal, deep down, the stories within it are there still. And metal painted to look like wood will never hold that memory.

Good Morning

Sometimes, I forget to say good morning,

in fact, I've gone years

in the bit hours of sudden woke, not knowing where I've
 been.

Sometimes, I leave me half-awake, dragged along in the
 tumult of a washing
machine that has no idea what stain or manner of thing it's
 trying to wash away.

So here now, in the waiting, I welcome home, me.

Crests

Cotton-top cresting rhythms
undergird opening laughter shells
sun shines through crisp, cold clarity
speckled glitter on a far-off horizon
adrift to eternity's puncture.
Always, the shoreline.
Always, the sea.

Light Splitter

Who am I when I hide curled,
cradling solar plexus gem? Power of eons
sequestered in calcite shards
dig into my soft fleshy womb
daring it to bleed.

Who am I when I take that gem,
encase it in gold,
buff the decorative facets?
And so am I to raise it high,
slow the roiling spectrum,
break light,
cleave color from saturated white?

Spin

Songs burrow beneath my fingernails
like the stardust dirt that congregates in my pores
and lives in the salted lines of haven drifts unmoored.

I was never meant to stay still, but spin into eons.

Silence

Step off, faces follow,
knees bend.
I walk on

through that room and the next one.
The train has passed; lay down the rumble,
I glide on.

My feet flit up over the uncrushed grass,
clicking beetle feet preening.
I fly on.

Sitting with you, the shadows flow
and before you speak,
I see you.

About the Author

JANETTE KENNEDY, MAEd, MFA frequently dreams of multi-textured colors connecting people. Her poetry has appeared at *Mothers Always Write* and on the *Tiferet Journal* community blog. Ever since she wrote her education thesis on using comics in the classroom, she has been fascinated by the intersection of language and visual art. At present, she tutors students with diverse needs and lives with her family in Tennessee.

About Unsolicited Press

Unsolicited Press based out of Portland, Oregon and focuses on the works of the unsung and underrepresented. As a womxn-owned, all-volunteer small publisher that doesn't worry about profits as much as championing exceptional literature, we have the privilege of partnering with authors skirting the fringes of the lit world. We've worked with emerging and award-winning authors such as Shann Ray, Amy Shimshon-Santo, Brook Bhagat, Kris Amos, and John W. Bateman.

Learn more at unsolicitedpress.com. Find us on twitter and instagram.

www.ingramcontent.com/pod-product-compliance
Lightning Source LLC
Chambersburg PA
CBHW031532120626
46545CB00005B/2107